once
a·day

40 DAYS TO EASTER

Kenneth Boa

with

John Allen Turner

ZONDERVAN®

ZONDERVAN

Once-A-Day 40 Days to Easter Devotional
Copyright © 2012 by Kenneth Boa

This title is also available as a Zondervan ebook.

Requests for information should be addressed to:
Zondervan, 3900 *Sparks Dr. SE, Grand Rapids, Michigan* 49546

Library of Congress Cataloging-in-Publication Data

Boa, Kenneth.
    Once-a-day 40 days to Easter devotional / written by
Kenneth Boa.
       p. cm. – (Once-a-day)
    ISBN 978-0-310-42132-0 (pbk.)
    1. Lent – Prayers and devotions. I. Title. II. Title: 40 days to
Easter devotional.
    BV85.B58 2013
    242'.34 – dc23
                                     2012028816

Cover design: *Jamie DeBruyn*
Interior design: *Sherri Hoffman and Jamie DeBruyn*

Printed in the United States of America

18 19 20 21 22 23 /QGP/ 16 15 14 13 12 11 10 9 8 7 6 5 4 3

CONTENTS

PREFACE

Lent and Our Preparation for Easter

"He was oppressed and afflicted, yet he did not open his mouth."   Isaiah 53:7

In his incarnation, Christ was "made in human likeness" (Philippians 2:7). He was a man, but more than a man; He was a servant, but more than a servant. His true glory was veiled in the weakness of his humanity.

The King of the universe, the Lord of glory, voluntarily became a pauper for our sake. He had to borrow a place to be born, a boat to preach from, a place to sleep, a donkey to ride upon, an upper room to use for the last supper and a tomb in which to be buried. He created the world, but the world did not know him. He was insulted, humiliated and rejected by the people he made. Yet he loved them even to the end, submitting to an agonizing and ignominious death. "Cursed is everyone who is hung on a pole" (Galatians 3:13; compare Deuteronomy 21:22–23). "And being found in appearance as a man, he humbled himself by becoming obedient to death—even death on a cross" (Philippians 2:8). It has been observed that only a divine being can accept death as obedience; for ordinary people it is a necessity.

Our Lord came to do the will of his Father and that obedience required a sacrifice (see Hebrews 10:5–9).

It was because of this obedience that "we have been made holy through the sacrifice of the body of Jesus Christ once for all" (Hebrews 10:10). Jesus was able to endure the pain and shame of the cross because of "the joy set before him" (Hebrews 12:2).

My friend John Alan Turner has crafted a wonderful series of reflections that will guide you through this Lenten season to prepare you for your celebration of the glory of the resurrection. Each of the 40 days has a series of Scriptures, a meditation and a prayer that will enrich and elevate your thoughts as you reflect on the Biblical meaning of this season and its relevance for your life today.

As John puts it, "Easter begins at Christmas. Joy to the world! For unto us a child is born; unto us a Son is given. Away in a manger. Silent night. This is where it begins. And yet we know the rest of the story. This baby was born for one primary purpose: to die."

Kenneth Boa, September 2012

day1

MATTHEW 27:50–51

And when Jesus had cried out again in a loud voice, he gave up his spirit. At that moment the curtain of the temple was torn in two from top to bottom.

HEBREWS 10:19–22

Therefore, brothers and sisters, since we have confidence to enter the Most Holy Place by the blood of Jesus, by a new and living way opened for us through the curtain, that is, his body, and since we have a great priest over the house of God, let us draw near to God with a sincere heart and with the full assurance that faith brings, having our hearts sprinkled to cleanse us from a guilty conscience and having our bodies washed with pure water.

READ ALSO GENESIS 3:17–24 AND COLOSSIANS 2:13–14.

MEDITATION

Since the fall of humans in the garden, people have lived with the knowledge that they are separated from their Creator. Jews in Jesus' day knew this full well, and in case they forgot, there was the curtain—the great, heavy curtain of blue, purple and scarlet thread and finely twisted linen (see Exodus 26:31). Four inches thick and so strong the historian Josephus said that horses tied to either side of it pulling could not tear it in two, it separated two rooms in the tabernacle.

Though the curtain was beautiful, its real purpose was not. It did not simply separate two rooms; it existed to bar entrance to God's holy place. It sent a message about the separation between God and people, serving as a reminder that no one was to ever approach God except in the limited ways he meticulously prescribed.

The curtain represented a closed door, open only to the high priest, and to him only once each year. And the only way he could survive entrance to that holy place was by the sprinkling of blood. The curtain constantly reminded God's people of their sin and the separation it brought between them and the One they longed for. The curtain, in one piece for so many years, communicated that God is holy, and his people, in their sin, were not.

As we enter this Lenten season, we prepare our hearts to celebrate the day the curtain was torn in two, from top to bottom, from God to human. Jesus was the true and perfect sacrifice, paying the penalty for all sin—once for all. The curtain no longer served a purpose. Let us solemnly remember Jesus' sacrifice on the day the holy place was opened to us.   ❖

PRAYER

Almighty Father, I rejoice in the knowledge that you actually want to be with me, a sinner, and to have me with you. I realize that your grace is far beyond my ability to comprehend. The sword of judgment that should have been held over me was broken on your Son and removed all barriers between us. Teach me how to come before you with the proper mix of humility and confidence. I confess my need for you and trust in what you have done for me. In Jesus' name I pray. Amen.

day2

GENESIS 6:11–13,17–18,22

Now the earth was corrupt in God's sight and was full of violence. God saw how corrupt the earth had become, for all the people on earth had corrupted their ways. So God said to Noah, "I am going to put an end to all people, for the earth is filled with violence because of them. I am surely going to destroy both them and the earth … I am going to bring floodwaters on the earth to destroy all life under the heavens, every creature that has the breath of life in it. Everything on earth will perish. But I will establish my covenant with you, and you will enter the ark—you and your sons and your wife and your sons' wives with you." … Noah did everything just as God commanded him.

READ ALSO 2 CORINTHIANS 5:17–19, 1 THESSALONIANS 1:9–10, HEBREWS 11:7 AND 2 PETER 2:5.

MEDITATION

Two extraordinary days of judgment have come in the history of our world. On the first, God destroyed all people, except one—Noah (with his family). On the second, the opposite occurred: God judged one man, Jesus, as a sacrifice and a savior for everyone else. Noah was a righteous man. He had been faithful. But he was not sinless. We know that all have sinned and fallen short of God's glory. And God had to know that Noah had and would again commit ugly sin. But God showed Noah magnificent favor. And that favor came in the form of a promise, a unilateral covenant, a one-sided showing of kindness so characteristic of the God of the Bible. "Enter the ark, and you and your family will be saved." Now God makes a similar offer to us: We will be saved as we enter into Christ. Jesus saves us from judgment and God's wrath, just as the ark saved Noah. The sacrifice made on the day we will celebrate as Good Friday was hideously painful, a cruel and demeaning punishment, the most wretched of deaths. But because of it, we and our families can be saved. That high price is a permanent reminder of the One who saved Noah and the One who saves us. Our appreciation is demonstrated by an obedient response, a total surrender and a handing over of the entirety of our lives. Noah got into the ark in obedience to God. We get into Jesus by the same obedience. And, like Noah, we are saved.   ♣

PRAYER

Gracious and merciful Father, you have made it clear that we cannot save ourselves. No one is perfect or even righteous; no one earns salvation. All of us fall short of your glory, and while it is true that some may live better lives, even the best cannot attain the perfection required in order to have fellowship with you. Thank you that, in your grace, you sent Jesus Christ to save me from the judgment to come. I believe in Jesus. I put my whole trust in him. And I ask that by your Spirit you would place me securely and safely in him. In Jesus' name I pray. Amen.

day3

GENESIS 11:1,4–7

Now the whole world had one language and a common speech ... Then they said, "Come, let us build ourselves a city, with a tower that reaches to the heavens, so that we may make a name for ourselves; otherwise we will be scattered over the face of the whole earth." But the LORD came down to see the city and the tower the people were building. The LORD said ... "Come, let us go down and confuse their language so they will not understand each other."

ACTS 2:5–8,11

Now there were staying in Jerusalem God-fearing Jews from every nation under heaven. When they heard this sound, a crowd came together in bewilderment, because each one heard their own language being spoken. Utterly amazed, they asked: "Aren't all these who are speaking Galileans? Then how is it that each of us hears them in our native language? ... We hear them declaring the wonders of God in our own tongues!"

READ ALSO EPHESIANS 4:3–6, REVELATION 5:9 AND 7:9–10.

MEDITATION

The very first command God gave to people was to multiply and fill the earth (see Genesis 1:28). Those who had known their Creator face to face would spread the goodness of his community throughout the whole earth. Sadly, it was not long before humans had fouled up the plan, built a city and let their pride lead them to believe they could build a tower so high it would bring them fame. In direct disobedience to the One who had given them life and breath and all things, they began to build. Proverbs 29:23 says that "pride brings a person low." And so these tower-builders were brought low and divided. And for centuries, this is how they lived, with many different languages, which formed national barriers and constant strife. But the plan of God has always been to reverse the curse of sin, a plan put in place with Jesus' sacrifice on the cross. At Pentecost, the language barriers were supernaturally removed, and those who had come together in Jerusalem to worship took the message of Jesus back home. It is our task too to spread the message of God's goodness to all people of all languages, lifting high the name of the One who, through his life, death and resurrection, brings us all back together again.   ♣

PRAYER

Lord of boundless love, your plans are perfect and your goodness extends to all who wish to receive it. Yet the whole of human history appears as a series of our attempts to make a name for ourselves in our own strength, on our own timetable and through our own efforts. Like the Tower of Babel, this always ends in confusion and division and chaos. But when we invite you into our lives, you turn our chaos into creative order. Grant me the wisdom to be more concerned with pleasing and obeying you and bringing honor to your name than I am about making a name for myself, for nothing on earth could ever compare to the incomparable pleasure of hearing you say, "Well done, good and faithful servant." In Christ's unifying name I pray. Amen.

day4

EXODUS 12:3,5–7,12–13

"Tell the whole community of Israel that ... each man is to take a lamb for his family ... The animals you choose must be year-old males without defect ... All the members of the community of Israel must slaughter them at twilight. Then they are to take some of the blood and put it on the sides and tops of the doorframes of the houses where they eat the lambs ... On that same night I will pass through Egypt and strike down every firstborn of both people and animals, and I will bring judgment on all the gods of Egypt. I am the LORD. The blood will be a sign for you on the houses where you are, and when I see the blood, I will pass over you. No destructive plague will touch you when I strike Egypt."

JOHN 1:29

The next day John saw Jesus coming toward him and said, "Look, the Lamb of God, who takes away the sin of the world!"

READ ALSO ISAIAH 53:7, 1 CORINTHIANS 5:7–8 AND REVELATION 5:11–12.

MEDITATION

God has been consistently clear: Deliverance requires sacrifice; salvation comes through the shed blood of another.

It was like that for Adam and Abraham, and it is like that for us. It certainly would have been an act of faith for God's people in Egypt to believe the message and do as God asked. It must have been a long, dark night that first Passover, families huddling together and wondering if God really would pass over them and keep them safe. Imagine the celebration as their fear turned to relief and doubt became trust.

Now roll the calendar ahead 1,500 years to Jesus celebrating the Passover with his closest friends. They ate the lamb and poured the wine, continuing their traditions throughout the meal. And then Jesus took the cup and said, "This cup is the new covenant in my blood, which is poured out for you" (Luke 22:20).

Just as the sacrificial lamb delivered the children of Abraham in Egypt, so also Jesus' blood delivers those who believe in him from the judgment of God. His death, which occurred at the same time as Passover lambs were being slaughtered in the temple, was no accident. His blood, in a sense, was applied over the "doorways" of our lives and, by our faith, now rescues us from death. Jesus' blood was shed for us all; what remains is for us to accept his sacrifice in faith and obedience.   ❖

PRAYER

Father, I believe the blood of the sinless One, the spotless Lamb of God, takes away the sins of the world, including mine. Thank you for forgiving my sin. Strengthen me in my faith and obedience. I invite you into more of my life and desire that I might become conformed to the image of your Son, in whose name I pray. Amen.

day5

EXODUS 19:5–8

[The LORD told Moses to tell the Israelites,] "'Now if you obey me fully and keep my covenant, then out of all nations you will be my treasured possession. Although the whole earth is mine, you will be for me a kingdom of priests and a holy nation.' These are the words you are to speak to the Israelites."

So Moses went back and summoned the elders of the people and set before them all the words the LORD had commanded him to speak. The people all responded together, "We will do everything the LORD has said." So Moses brought their answer back to the LORD.

ROMANS 3:23

For all have sinned and fall short of the glory of God.

READ ALSO GALATIANS 3:23–25, PHILIPPIANS 3:8–9, ROMANS 4:23–25 AND JOHN 5:39–40.

MEDITATION

God must have known that the law he gave to his people through Moses was too difficult for a sinful people to follow. And so, it would have come as no surprise to him that they failed. They turned away from God and looked for their ultimate fulfillment not in him but in other things. A holy and just God cannot lower his standards. In the fallen world in which we live, there developed a great divide, a separation between God and humans. But the God who works all things together for our good provided a way for everyone to become his, a way for all of us to meet *his* standards. And he made it simple (though we must not confuse simple with easy). God sent his Son as a sacrifice. In order for Jesus to begin the process of reforming God's image in us, he had to become one of us, yet remain perfectly righteous. And he had to pay the ultimate penalty for all of our sin, suffering on the cross, experiencing for unbearable hours all of the pain that sin brings. And that is what he did. ✤

PRAYER

Holy Father, you are perfect and just in all your ways, and it is only in you that I can find true life. Protect me from the subtle forms of idolatry that infiltrate my heart, that I find myself serving and worshiping even as they lead me to frustration and despair. You and you alone must occupy the center of my being. I am grateful that when I do succumb to the sins of disobedience, your grace reaches further than my rebellion. Thank you for sending your Son to rescue me—to keep the law and to die as a sinless sacrifice for my wayward thoughts, feelings and acts. Teach me to rest in your righteousness and pursue you above all else. In Christ's holy name. Amen.

day6

EXODUS 32:1,7,10,30

When the people saw that Moses was so long in coming down from the mountain, they gathered around Aaron and said, "Come, make us gods who will go before us. As for this fellow Moses who brought us up out of Egypt, we don't know what has happened to him." ...

Then the LORD said to Moses, "Go down, because your people, whom you brought up out of Egypt, have become corrupt ... Now leave me alone so that my anger may burn against them and that I may destroy them." ...

The next day Moses said to the people, "You have committed a great sin. But now I will go up to the LORD; perhaps I can make atonement for your sin."

LEVITICUS 9:7

Moses said to Aaron, "Come to the altar and sacrifice your sin offering and your burnt offering and make atonement for yourself and the people; sacrifice the offering that is for the people and make atonement for them, as the LORD has commanded."

READ ALSO LEVITICUS 9:23–24 AND 1 JOHN 2:1–2.

MEDITATION

Even a cursory reading of the Bible shows that no one has ever been truly faithful to God. Everywhere you look you see people sinning, turning away from God and then crying out for mercy when they find themselves in trouble. God knew this would happen and, in his mercy, built a solemn and precious day into the Jewish calendar, the Day of Atonement. On this day, the high priest would make sacrificial offerings for himself and for all the people. Once these rituals were complete, all the sins of all the Jewish people would be ceremonially transferred to a goat, and the goat would be released into the wilderness.

But what about us? We continue to turn away from God, day in and day out, our sin mounting higher and higher until it becomes too large to ignore. What can we do? Is there some ritual or ceremony that can take our sins away? No, but we have a High Priest, Jesus Christ, the Righteous One, who lived a sinless life and died a sacrificial death, taking our sin upon himself and in exchange offering his righteousness to us. Because of him, and him only, we are forgiven, free, clean and able to live — for all eternity.   ❖

PRAYER

Loving Lord, I thank you that you sent your Son into this world to be my High Priest. Thank you for his sinless life that enabled him to make atonement for my sin and for the sins of the whole world. Thank you for his death, for the shedding of his blood that saves me and makes me holy in your sight. Help me now to enjoy the peace of knowing that my sins are removed from me through the sacrifice on the cross of Jesus Christ my Lord. Amen.

day7

LEVITICUS 16:20–21

"When Aaron has finished making atonement for the Most Holy Place, the tent of meeting and the altar, he shall bring forward the live goat. He is to lay both hands on the head of the live goat and confess over it all the wickedness and rebellion of the Israelites — all their sins — and put them on the goat's head. He shall send the goat away into the wilderness."

2 CORINTHIANS 5:21

God made him who had no sin to be sin for us, so that in him we might become the righteousness of God.

1 TIMOTHY 2:5–6

For there is one God and one mediator between God and mankind, the man Christ Jesus, who gave himself as a ransom for all people.

READ ALSO PSALM 103:9–12 AND HEBREWS 9:11–14.

MEDITATION

For more than 1,000 years, the Jewish sacrificial system had been firmly in place, sometimes strictly followed, sometimes not adhered to at all. But the Jews knew that the only way to pay for the sins of the people required loss of life (blood) and the actions of a priest. By Jesus' time, the system had become terribly distorted. Two groups fought over how sacrifices should be made and where people could buy those sacrifices. This was displeasing to God.

Prophecy spoke of the Messiah to come, and the time had come. God sent his Son into the world to be both priest and sacrifice—to be the final sacrifice and put the priests permanently out of the sacrifice business. From the cross Jesus, the perfect Man and the perfect high priest, while offering the perfect sacrifice (his own spotless blood), prayed, "Father, forgive them" (Luke 23:34). God raised him from the dead to show his acceptance of this perfect sacrifice.

Now, just as Jesus is the one who is our legal advocate for our crime, he is also the one making the sacrifice and paying the penalty for us. He is the sacrifice. Only the One who had lived a sinless life could have done this. Today, Jesus is our high priest, and we must never let anyone (not a priest or a saint or a pastor) come between us and God. And our heavenly, holy and human high priest is our assurance of eternal salvation.   ❖

PRAYER

Lord Jesus, you are our great high priest. Only you could provide the sacrifice necessary for the cleansing of our sins. I thank you for your love, shown most clearly in offering yourself as a sinless sacrifice on my behalf. You endured degradation, malice, betrayal, agony and death so that I, who would have no hope of ever being acceptable to you, can receive forgiveness and acceptance. I come to you in my uncleanness and corruption, asking for your forgiveness. I humbly thank you for the gift of life that I could never merit on my own. May I never forget the awful price you paid to make it possible. Teach me the dignity of offering myself to you in return, as a living sacrifice. In your holy name I pray. Amen.

day8

NUMBERS 21:4–9

[The Israelites] traveled from Mount Hor along the route to the Red Sea, to go around Edom. But the people grew impatient on the way; they spoke against God and against Moses, and said, "Why have you brought us up out of Egypt to die in the wilderness? There is no bread! There is no water! And we detest this miserable food!"

Then the LORD sent venomous snakes among them; they bit the people and many Israelites died. The people came to Moses and said, "We sinned when we spoke against the LORD and against you. Pray that the LORD will take the snakes away from us." So Moses prayed for the people.

The LORD said to Moses, "Make a snake and put it up on a pole; anyone who is bitten can look at it and live." So Moses made a bronze snake and put it up on a pole. Then when anyone was bitten by a snake and looked at the bronze snake, they lived.

JOHN 3:14–16

[Jesus said,] "Just as Moses lifted up the snake in the wilderness, so the Son of Man must be lifted up, that everyone who believes may have eternal life in him."

For God so loved the world that he gave his one and only Son, that whoever believes in him shall not perish but have eternal life.

READ ALSO JOHN 12:31–33 AND PHILIPPIANS 2:8–11.

MEDITATION

Buried deep inside the book of Numbers is an obscure story about snakes and the strange way God went about saving his people from their poisonous bites. But this is actually a story about Jesus and about us. God could have taken the snakes away, but he chose not to. Why? Because he wanted the people to trust him; gazing up at that bronze serpent demonstrated that trust.

Jesus retold the story from Numbers when Nicodemus came to him, failing to understand how a person could ever enter the kingdom of God. Jesus clarified his role, saying the "Son of Man must be lifted up" just as "Moses lifted up the snake in the wilderness" (John 3:14). All Nicodemus had to do was believe in Jesus, and he too would have eternal life.

This Jesus, on whom we fix our eyes, is the author and perfecter of our faith. By gazing at him, we come to know him and are transformed by him. Jesus did not come to take away our poisonous snakes. He came so that we could, by fixing our gaze on him, be healed from their venomous bite—made whole and healthy, set right again with God.

✣

PRAYER

Lord Jesus, I fix my eyes on you and gaze at you in your glory. I give thanks for your mercy, patience and kindness and for your willingness to endure my wandering. I confess that keeping on the right path is difficult. By the power of your Spirit, I pray that I will hold fast to you not only in times of adversity but also in times of ease. In your healing name I pray. Amen.

day 9

DEUTERONOMY 17:14–15

When you enter the land the LORD your God is giving you and have taken possession of it and settled in it, and you say, "Let us set a king over us like all the nations around us," be sure to appoint over you a king the LORD your God chooses.

1 SAMUEL 8:4–7

So all the elders of Israel gathered together and came to Samuel at Ramah. They said to him, "You are old, and your sons do not follow your ways; now appoint a king to lead us, such as all the other nations have." ... [Samuel] prayed to the LORD. And the LORD told him: "Listen to all that the people are saying to you; it is not you they have rejected, but they have rejected me as their king."

JOHN 19:14–15

It was the day of Preparation of the Passover; it was about noon. "Here is your king," Pilate said to the Jews. But they shouted, "Take him away! Take him away! Crucify him!" "Shall I crucify your king?" Pilate asked. "We have no king but Caesar," the chief priests answered.

*READ ALSO MATTHEW 6:10, 27:27–29 AND 41–42,
    AND REVELATION 19:16.*

MEDITATION

When we reject God as our King, we repeat an age-old cycle of sin, discipline, repentance, restoration and sin again. God longs to be our one and only King, but we want to follow a human; so, sadly, God often gives us what we ask for.

For the Israelites, king after king after king failed to produce a people who could represent God's kingdom virtues and values on earth. Some kings were better than others, but not one was able to rule the people of God in the manner of God. Eventually, God had only one choice: He sent his own Son into the world to deliver the people from their enemies. This One would be "the King of the Jews." This King came in the form of a servant. He allowed those he came to rule to mock and ridicule him. But, as difficult as this is to imagine, it was through the bloodied, disfigured and crucified King that the will of the Father was finally accomplished, and we are brought into victory and blessing.

✤

PRAYER

Lord Jesus, you and you alone are worthy of being called "King." You are the Lamb who was slain whose blood purchased for God the people from every tribe and tongue and nation. And I join with the saints of old in praying, "Maranatha! Lord, come quickly!" Come, Lord Jesus. Amen.

day 10

PSALM 22:1–5

My God, my God, why have you forsaken me? Why are you so far from saving me, so far from my cries of anguish? My God, I cry out by day, but you do not answer, by night, but I find no rest. Yet you are enthroned as the Holy One; you are the one Israel praises. In you our ancestors put their trust; they trusted and you delivered them. To you they cried out and were saved; in you they trusted and were not put to shame.

MEDITATION

God never promised that we would be exempt from affliction; rather, suffering is part of our lot in a fallen world. However, there is hope because, though he does not always deliver us *from* suffering, he promises to deliver and transform us *through* it if we rely on his resources instead of our own. In such times of suffering, we can know for sure that we are not alone. In the midst of our pain, God promises to never leave us or abandon us.

Therefore, when we grieve, we do not grieve like the world does; we grieve with hope, knowing that God is often revealed most clearly in the midst of our trials. God will never despise us or hide his face from us. When we cry for help, he will hear and will enable us to endure. The certainty of his companionship in the midst of our afflictions allows us to view them as a means to a greater end. Our suffering is accomplishing something in us, forging within us the character of the One in whose image we are made. Because of Christ, even our catastrophes have purpose. God is preparing our character for the time when we will see him face to face.   ❖

PRAYER

Lord of all creation, you have shown me that I will have tribulation in this world. But you have counseled me to take courage because you have overcome the world and have promised to never leave or forsake me. Grant me the grace to hold fast to the truths of the gospel, to the Person and work of Christ, and to the power of the Spirit. May I hope in your promises, confessing that I am but a stranger and exile in this world, reveling in the love you have shown me and extending that love to others. Teach me to exult in my tribulations, knowing that difficulties bring about perseverance, character and a hope that does not disappoint. And may I always remember that I am headed for a glorious and eternal future with you that cannot be compared to the temporary struggles of this world. In your steadfast name I pray. Amen.

day11

ISAIAH 53:3–6

He was despised and rejected by mankind, a man of suffering, and familiar with pain. Like one from whom people hide their faces he was despised, and we held him in low esteem.

Surely he took up our pain and bore our suffering, yet we considered him punished by God, stricken by him, and afflicted. But he was pierced for our transgressions, he was crushed for our iniquities; the punishment that brought us peace was on him, and by his wounds we are healed. We all, like sheep, have gone astray, each of us has turned to our own way; and the LORD has laid on him the iniquity of us all.

MEDITATION

The human condition is desperate. It is for this reason that Jesus had to suffer. Just as foolish sheep wander off, we too turn our backs and walk away from God to our own detriment. We all do it. This is why it was important for Jesus to bear the sin of "us all" on his shoulders. But suffering was not the end of his story. Isaiah speaks in the future tense as well, beyond the excruciating torment of the cross, about a time when Jesus would "see the light of life" and the satisfaction in seeing his reward: our justification.

Jesus is the perfect fulfillment of this Old Testament prophecy. It was Jesus' clear purpose in coming to this earth that he would not be served, but would do the serving and give his life as a ransom for us—because we were held in captivity, wandering sheep penned up by an evil captor, but now freed by a gentle Savior. Jesus did not suffer on the cross in spite of who he was, but rather precisely because of who he was. Our redemption was his mission. Service and sacrifice were (and are) part of his nature, as they should become part of ours. The example Jesus set of servanthood transcends any example people have ever seen before or ever will see. This other-centeredness, as it was so clearly modeled by our Savior, is now our foremost calling. And he promises that this is how we will find true life.   ✣

PRAYER

God of eternity, you saw the beginning and you see the end. Your plan has always been good, though I often fail to recognize it as such. As I look to you with love and awe, I am learning to view my circumstances and challenges in this life with courage, knowing that you have my destiny in your hands. My confidence is in your promises. I know that my future is secure in you. I ask for a greater understanding of your purpose for me on this earth and your guidance as I share your Good News with the people I encounter during this earthly pilgrimage as I await my eternal home with you. I pray this in the name of the One who loves me and gave himself for me. Amen.

day 12

JUDGES 2:18–19

Whenever the LORD raised up a judge for them, he was with the judge and saved them out of the hands of their enemies as long as the judge lived; for the LORD relented because of their groaning under those who oppressed and afflicted them. But when the judge died, the people returned to ways even more corrupt than those of their ancestors, following other gods and serving and worshiping them. They refused to give up their evil practices and stubborn ways.

MATTHEW 1:20–21

An angel of the Lord appeared to him in a dream and said, "Joseph son of David, do not be afraid to take Mary home as your wife, because what is conceived in her is from the Holy Spirit. She will give birth to a son, and you are to give him the name Jesus, because he will save his people from their sins."

READ ALSO PSALM 18:2–3, JOHN 8:34–36 AND COLOSSIANS 1:13–14.

MEDITATION

God has always had a plan to save his people and deliver them from their sins. The judges first modeled the role of deliverer, but their ministry was always temporary. Judges had no long-term ability to deliver the people from their enemies in any final sense. They could not keep people from sinning (or even keep from sinning themselves). But Jesus could. His name, in Hebrew, means "Yahweh saves." There could be no clearer message. God is a God who saves his people.

The problem the people in Jesus' time had in receiving Christ is the same problem we face now. We all want a Deliverer, someone to help us out of our financial struggles, our troubled relationships, our sickness. But none of us seems quite so desperate to be saved from the dominion of darkness, from sin.

Let us not forget during this Lenten season that our God has control over all powers and authorities, over all the spiritual forces in the world and over all the rebellious people throughout the course of history. Our God hears us when we cry for help and will bring us safely into his heavenly kingdom. Nothing can stop him from saving us except our own foolish rejection of the Deliverer himself.   ❖

PRAYER

God of mercy and grace, until you intervened, I was on a path that led only to disappointment, emptiness and death. But because you are merciful, you opened my eyes so I could see my spiritual bankruptcy — the true nature of my condition and the depth of my real need. When I cried out to you for deliverance, you saved me. Only then could I reach out and lay hold of your grace and your transforming power. I thank you for my salvation. You are my deliverer and my hope for this life and for the life to come. In your Son's name I pray. Amen.

day 13

2 SAMUEL 7:4–5,16

That night the word of the LORD came to Nathan, saying: "Go and tell my servant David, 'This is what the LORD says: … Your house and your kingdom will endure forever before me; your throne will be established forever.'"

ISAIAH 9:6–7

For to us a child is born, to us a son is given, and the government will be on his shoulders. And he will be called Wonderful Counselor, Mighty God, Everlasting Father, Prince of Peace. Of the greatness of his government and peace there will be no end. He will reign on David's throne and over his kingdom, establishing and upholding it with justice and righteousness from that time on and forever. The zeal of the LORD Almighty will accomplish this.

LUKE 1:30–33

But the angel said to [Mary], "Do not be afraid, Mary; you have found favor with God. You will conceive and give birth to a son, and you are to call him Jesus. He will be great and will be called the Son of the Most High. The Lord God will give him the throne of his father David, and he will reign over Jacob's descendants forever; his kingdom will never end."

READ ALSO MATTHEW 12:22–23 AND REVELATION 11:15.

DAY 13 32

MEDITATION

The title "Son of David" carried weighty significance for the
Jews of Jesus' time. They had long awaited a Messiah who
would come from David's line and fulfill the promises of Isaiah.
David was a great and beloved king, but David signified something that could not be represented by anyone else: the glory
of Israel. Under David, the Israelites were unified and free. David led the kingdom to liberation from its enemies, prosperity
and greatness, in devotion to God. For generations, no one in
Israel would ever forget what it was like when David was king.

By the time of Jesus' coming, Israel's glory was long gone.
But the people would never forget that glory. While Jesus
lived on earth, many scholars and religious authorities failed
to recognize him as the fulfillment of this Davidic promise
because they missed a link in the line that was drawn from
David to Jesus. But Matthew did not miss it. He put it right at
the front of his Gospel. Those 17 verses contain some unusual
names for a genealogy, names like Boaz and Ruth, Judah and
Tamar, Rahab and Bathsheba—women, sinners, outsiders.
And now we all, outsiders that we are, can come to Jesus and
find that freedom, that unity and that glory.   ❖

PRAYER

*God and Father, all glory, honor and praise are due to you
alone not merely because of who you are but because of
what you have done. You destroyed the yoke of sin and slav-
ery that held me captive. I praise you for this gift of acceptance that overcomes the bondage of sin and unites us all
together now into one body, with Jesus, the son of David,
as the head. I pray this in his name. Amen.*

day14

ISAIAH 53:11

After he has suffered, he will see the light of life and be satisfied.

JOHN 10:17

The reason my Father loves me is that I lay down my life—only to take it up again.

READ ALSO LUKE 2:21–35.

MEDITATION

Easter begins at Christmas. Joy to the world! For unto us a child is born; unto us a Son is given. Away in a manger. Silent night. This is where it begins. And yet we know the rest of the story. This baby was born for one primary purpose: to die.

Surely Mary and Joseph would have been worried, as all first-time parents are, that their newborn would be healthy. They probably experienced relief that he survived his unorthodox birth and lived to his eighth day when they could present him in the temple. And, though they had not been told exactly what it meant, they believed the angel's words—that this baby would somehow save his people from their sins. The angel did not tell them that he would cause trouble. And so it must have come as some shock to hear the words of the old man Simeon. Their son, their only son, whom they loved, would bring pain. People would say terrible things against him. As Jesus grew, he understood this, hinting to his friends that his destiny would not be a pleasant one. But they failed to understand. Eventually, he stated it explicitly. He would be condemned and murdered, but he would return. One of his closest friends shouted, "Never!" But Jesus was resolute. This Christmas baby was born to be subjected to brutality and humiliation. He would lay down his life so that he could bring eternal life to us all. Joy to the world, indeed.   ❖

PRAYER

Sovereign Lord, I am mystified by the incarnation of your Son. God taking on flesh. The Creator of all becoming one of us. This is astonishing, too marvelous for words. You willingly offered the life of your Son in exchange for ours. You transferred our sin to him and his righteousness to us. Knowing he would be betrayed, rejected and murdered by the people he came to save, he still came. He willingly became the sacrifice by dying on the cross. He overcame death. May I always be thankful for your glorious gift and recall the awful price you paid to make it possible. In Christ's name I pray. Amen.

day15

GENESIS 2:16–17

And the Lord God commanded the man, "You are free to eat from any tree in the garden; but you must not eat from the tree of the knowledge of good and evil, for when you eat from it you will certainly die."

GENESIS 3:6–7

When the woman saw that the fruit of the tree was good for food and pleasing to the eye, and also desirable for gaining wisdom, she took some and ate it. She also gave some to her husband, who was with her, and he ate it. Then the eyes of both of them were opened, and they realized they were naked; so they sewed fig leaves together and made coverings for themselves.

ROMANS 5:17

If, by the trespass of the one man, death reigned through that one man, how much more will those who receive God's abundant provision of grace and of the gift of righteousness reign in life through the one man, Jesus Christ!

READ ALSO ROMANS 8:1, 1 CORINTHIANS 15:22 AND 2 CORINTHIANS 5:17.

MEDITATION

The record of human history can be viewed as the story of the conflict between the power of sin and the power of

God's grace. God graciously begins by planting a garden and placing two people, Adam and Eve, there. Through their sin, evil invades and corrupts their place of blessing, forcing them away from God's presence. God's grace responds by promising to ultimately destroy the power of evil. Sin retaliates by bringing violence and bloodshed into the world and multiplying it throughout the generations. God's grace offers a childless couple a baby. Sin enslaves the children of Abraham in Egypt. Grace delivers them through the Red Sea. On and on the story goes. Sin and grace wrestle to see which side will have the upper hand. But little by little, it becomes clear that grace is establishing its position, gaining the upper hand, preparing to land its decisive and crushing blow.

Grace, in the person of Jesus Christ, takes on human flesh. Sin lashes out, trying to kill the child. Grace finds a safe place for him in Egypt. Sin tempts Jesus. Grace defeats temptation. The blind see. The lame walk. Demons shriek. Sin musters its strength for one final battle, but grace wins in the most astonishing turn of events. There is One over whom sin has no power and over whom death has no hold. Only he is able to release those held hostage to the sin Adam allowed into the world. ♣

PRAYER

Almighty Father, thank you for leading me toward my final home with you. I pray all of this through the power and strength of Jesus Christ my Lord and Savior. Amen.

day16

LUKE 4:1–12

Jesus, full of the Holy Spirit, left the Jordan and was led by the Spirit into the wilderness, where for forty days he was tempted by the devil. He ate nothing during those days, and at the end of them he was hungry.

The devil said to him, "If you are the Son of God, tell this stone to become bread."

Jesus answered, "It is written: 'Man shall not live on bread alone.'"

The devil led him up to a high place and showed him in an instant all the kingdoms of the world. And he said to him, "I will give you all their authority and splendor; it has been given to me, and I can give it to anyone I want to. If you worship me, it will all be yours."

Jesus answered, "It is written: 'Worship the Lord your God and serve him only.'"

The devil led him to Jerusalem and had him stand on the highest point of the temple. "If you are the Son of God," he said, "throw yourself down from here. For it is written: 'He will command his angels concerning you to guard you carefully; they will lift you up in their hands, so that you will not strike your foot against a stone.'"

Jesus answered, "It is said: 'Do not put the Lord your God to the test.'"

HEBREWS 4:14–16

Therefore, since we have a great high priest who has ascended into heaven, Jesus the Son of God, let us hold firmly to the faith we profess. For we do not have a high priest who is unable to empathize with our weaknesses, but we have one who has been tempted in every way, just as we are—yet he did not sin. Let us then approach God's throne of grace with confidence, so that we may receive mercy and find grace to help us in our time of need.

MEDITATION

Immediately after his baptism and the announcement of his public ministry, Jesus found himself in the wilderness, alone and vulnerable. Armed with nothing but the Scripture he had buried in his heart, Jesus faced the enemy.

If the severity of our temptations is dependent on the threat we pose against the forces of darkness, we can assume that Christ's temptation was more than just a battle of words. In fact, this was an assault.

Years later, in the Garden of Gethsemane, Jesus was alone and again vulnerable. There he wrestled with his own desire to avoid that which his Father had planned since before the beginning of time. "Take this cup from me," he prayed, but ended with, "Not my will, but yours be done" (Luke 22:42). His trial in the wilderness trained him well. He remains strong to this day, empathizing with our weaknesses and strengthening us to say, when we pray, "Not my will, but yours." ❖

PRAYER

God of all comfort and strength, you offer yourself as the ultimate resource for me when I find myself lonely and vulnerable. Teach me the wisdom of quickly turning to you in those times, guide me to look to you for my needs and to fully submit myself to your good will for my life. Only then will I come to know the peace that surpasses all understanding and guards my heart and mind in Christ Jesus. Amen.

day 17

DEUTERONOMY 30:19–20

This day I call the heavens and the earth as witnesses against you that I have set before you life and death, blessings and curses. Now choose life, so that you and your children may live and that you may love the LORD your God, listen to his voice, and hold fast to him. For the LORD is your life, and he will give you many years in the land he swore to give to your fathers, Abraham, Isaac and Jacob.

JOHN 10:7–10

Therefore Jesus said again, "Very truly I tell you, I am the gate for the sheep ... I am the gate; whoever enters through me will be saved. They will come in and go out, and find pasture. The thief comes only to steal and kill and destroy; I have come that they may have life, and have it to the full."

READ ALSO PSALM 23 AND COLOSSIANS 3:1–4.

MEDITATION

Jesus was very clear about why he had come into this world. It wasn't to pass judgment. It wasn't to congratulate good people who followed the rules. Jesus Christ came into the world to bring life, an abundant life that fills us to overflowing. This has always been God's intention toward his people. God created us to experience a life of fulfillment and promise. It is his trademark to give us more than we need, to flood our lives with blessings.

Yet God's people have consistently chosen to walk a path of disobedience and rebellion, a path that leads to death. But God was not willing to leave us on that path. He sent his Son to bear the curse of our sins for us, to pay the price for our sins, once for all. God made it possible for us to get off the road the leads to destruction and onto the road that leads to eternal life. Jesus offers all those who enter this new life through him a forever life in the presence of God. Let us remember that he is not only the provider of this life, he is our life.   ✤

PRAYER

God of grace and truth, you have revealed your will and your ways in your Word. In its pages I discover truths I would never learn anywhere else. Thank you for this eternal life that is now mine because of your divine intervention in my life. Help me to overcome my spiritual and moral inertia that keeps me from hearing your voice and walking in your ways. May I hold your words in my heart so that I will not succumb to temptation and sin, but be increasingly honoring to you. Give me the strength to set my mind and heart on things above, where Christ is. Help me to find my life in you and be defined by your truth rather than by the lies of this world. Strengthen me in my unconditional commitment to you. I love you and know that you first loved me. In Christ's name I pray. Amen.

day 18

LAMENTATIONS 1:1; 3:21–23

How deserted lies the city [of Jerusalem], once so full of people! How like a widow is she, who once was great among the nations! She who was queen among the provinces has now become a slave ...

Yet this I call to mind and therefore I have hope: Because of the LORD's great love we are not consumed, for his compassions never fail. They are new every morning; great is your faithfulness.

LUKE 19:41–42

As [Jesus] approached Jerusalem and saw the city, he wept over it and said, "If you, even you, had only known on this day what would bring you peace—but now it is hidden from your eyes."

REVELATION 21:3–4

And I heard a loud voice from the throne saying, "Look! God's dwelling place is now among the people, and he will dwell with them. They will be his people, and God himself will be with them and be their God. 'He will wipe every tear from their eyes. There will be no more death' or mourning or crying or pain, for the old order of things has passed away."

READ ALSO 2 CORINTHIANS 1:3–5.

MEDITATION

Jesus promised his followers many things: peace, joy, abundant life, forgiveness of sins, a secure union with him. One thing he did not promise, however, is a pain-free life here on earth. Rather, he warned us that we would have trouble in this world. That may not be fair, but life stopped being fair when Adam and Eve ate the forbidden fruit in the Garden of Eden. The ripple effects of that sin continue with us to this day.

Since that day in the garden, life has been filled with pain. But one of the most remarkable things about the Christian faith — one of the things that sets Christianity apart from other world religions — is that our God feels our pain with us. He weeps with us. Our tears matter to him. And one day, he promises, we will weep no longer. Death will disappear and no one will feel pain. Until then, Jesus has sent the Holy Spirit to be our Comforter. It is as we seek his face in the midst of our trials that our sorrow, even now, can be turned to joy.   ❖

PRAYER

Faithful Father, when I place this life in the context of your life, my story becomes a sentence in a paragraph in a chapter of the story you have been writing since before the beginning of time. Only in that light can I see that you are indeed causing all things to work together for good to those who love you and are called according to your purposes. Give me the perspective to see that the sufferings of this present time are not worthy to be compared with the glory that is to be revealed to your children in Christ. In his name I pray. Amen.

day 19

MATTHEW 11:19

"The Son of Man came eating and drinking, and they say, 'Here is a glutton and a drunkard, a friend of tax collectors and sinners.'"

LUKE 7:36–39

When one of the Pharisees invited Jesus to have dinner with him, he went to the Pharisee's house and reclined at the table. A woman in that town who lived a sinful life learned that Jesus was eating at the Pharisee's house, so she came there with an alabaster jar of perfume. As she stood behind him at his feet weeping, she began to wet his feet with her tears. Then she wiped them with her hair, kissed them and poured perfume on them.

When the Pharisee who had invited him saw this, he said to himself, "If this man were a prophet, he would know who is touching him and what kind of woman she is — that she is a sinner."

LUKE 5:29–32

Then Levi held a great banquet for Jesus at his house, and a large crowd of tax collectors and others were eating with them. But the Pharisees and the teachers of the law who belonged to their sect complained to his disciples, "Why do you eat and drink with tax collectors and sinners?"

Jesus answered them, "It is not the healthy who need a doctor, but the sick. I have not come to call the righteous, but sinners to repentance."

READ ALSO LUKE 15:1–2 AND 19:1–7.

MEDITATION

Sin is awful. It separates us from God. The religious leaders of Jesus' time got at least this much right. But they had worked it all out in their own favor, exempting themselves from any consequences. And in so doing, they built their own system, a system of insiders and outsiders divided by arbitrary laws God had not written that were enforced by real guards.

The outcasts — the sick, the ceremonially unclean, the sinful, the drunkards, the prostitutes, the Samaritan half-breeds and the tax collectors (those who lined their own pockets for the sake of the Romans and at the expense of their fellow Jews) — these people had little in common save one thing: None of them were allowed entrance to the temple. They were not allowed to approach God. Yet it is with these people that Jesus finds himself, even seems to seek out. He dines with sinners and tax collectors, lets a prostitute wash his feet, refuses to agree to the stoning of an adulteress, touches lepers and a bleeding woman! For a Jew who strictly obeyed the law, these behaviors were completely unsuitable.

Unless, through his actions, Jesus is saying something, making a statement about what God thinks of those in authority who hide their own sins behind robes and titles while exposing the sins of others and prohibiting them from worshiping God. Jesus did not judge the sinners or the unclean. He loved and respected them. He offered them acceptance and said that he (not the traditions that stood against them) was the only way to God. And because he spoke with authority and walked in integrity (he hid no sins under his robes), many believed him. ❖

PRAYER

Holy Lord, you dwell on a high and hallowed place. Holiness is in all you say and do, and holiness is what eludes me most. I am a sinner, and I have sinned in my thoughts, my feelings and my actions. I live in a sinful world among sinful people. And yet you sent your Son to redeem us. He was known as a friend of sinners. People who were nothing like him liked him and were drawn to him. You chose to sanctify me in him, to set me apart from my sin. You accepted me as I am and promised that I do not have to remain as I am. Rather, through the power of your Holy Spirit, you have begun changing me in ways I could never change by myself. All glory and honor to you, Lord. In Jesus' name I pray. Amen.

day20

JOHN 15:5–8

"I am the vine; you are the branches. If you remain in me and I in you, you will bear much fruit; apart from me you can do nothing. If you do not remain in me, you are like a branch that is thrown away and withers; such branches are picked up, thrown into the fire and burned. If you remain in me and my words remain in you, ask whatever you wish, and it will be done for you. This is to my Father's glory, that you bear much fruit, showing yourselves to be my disciples."

MEDITATION

The promised land had been filled with grape vines, with branches everywhere, weighed down by enormous bunches of fruit. The grapevine had become a symbol of the people of Israel, and gold clusters of grapes hung over the temple gate. Those listening to Jesus knew that Israel was the vine that God took from Egypt and planted in the promised land. They knew from the Psalms, from Isaiah and Jeremiah and Ezekiel that the vine had been a disappointment when it failed to produce fruit. It was a symbol of their intended purpose, but it was also a reminder of their failure. Leaves and fruit on a grapevine were good, but branches that did not produce were not strong enough to build anything with; their only use was as firewood, and God had told them this.

So when Jesus opened his mouth to speak of a vine on this day, they may have been holding their breath. Or they may have noticed that he said he was the "true" vine, and that may have stung a little. But if they listened closely, they would see that Jesus was giving them another chance.

Branches that produce fruit must come from a reliable vine. Here stood that reliable source giving the people of Israel an opportunity to overcome failure, to live to glorify God again. They had been chosen by Jesus, their source of strength (see John 15:16). If they would remain in loving union with him and find their life purpose, their strength and their deepest pleasure in him, they could produce something that would last forever and be truly significant. If they understood what he was saying, they would see that this was an offer as gigantic as a six-pound bunch of grapes. And if we are wise, it is ours to see it this way too.   ♣

PRAYER

Lord Jesus, you are the true vine, and without you I can do nothing of lasting value. As a branch derives its life from the vine, may I remain in you and draw upon your resources rather than attempting to live in my own power. I know that it is only as I maintain this connection with you that I will be able to bear fruit that will endure and glorify your name. Teach me the joy of living in utter dependence on you, of seeing you as the conduit of real life. It is only from you that I draw the nourishment necessary to be sustained in this dry and weary land. Grant that I may know you in a personal way, and may that growing knowledge create in me a thirst to share you with others. As I grow in my love for you, may I also grow in my obedience to you so that I will be known as your true disciple. In your life-giving name I pray. Amen.

day21

LUKE 14:11

"For all those who exalt themselves will be humbled, and those who humble themselves will be exalted."

MARK 10:43–45

"Whoever wants to become great among you must be your servant, and whoever wants to be first must be slave of all. For even the Son of Man did not come to be served, but to serve, and to give his life as a ransom for many."

JOHN 5:30

"By myself I can do nothing; I judge only as I hear, and my judgment is just, for I seek not to please myself but him who sent me."

READ ALSO PHILIPPIANS 2:5–11.

MEDITATION

Jesus was criticized, rejected, slandered, misunderstood, plotted against, betrayed, denied and abused by family, friends and disciples, by Jewish religious leaders and by Romans. He chose identification with sinners and lived in poverty and obscurity for most of his 33 years. As his ministry progressed, Jesus faced increasing levels of hostility and opposition. Yet, he knew who and whose he was, and his relationship with the Father gave him the power and security to love and serve others. He was never defined and bound by the opinions of those around him.

The humility of Jesus Christ was an extraordinary reflection of an absolute dependence on and submission to God. We see this in his baptism, as a dove descends. Doves were the sacrifice poor people offered. Jesus identifies with the poor, the lowly, the outcast.

For us, humility is the mark of true repentance, evidence of a transformed life. Our flesh and our pride chafe against humility, so we are forced to learn it through suffering, through forgiving those who wrong us and by seeing these incidents as opportunities to grow. As we do, we begin to develop a teachable spirit, a willingness to seek wise counsel and submission to authority. As we join John the Baptist in saying, "He must become greater; I must become less" (John 3:30), we learn the wisdom of humility and stand in awe of our Lord's amazing grace. ❧

PRAYER

God of heaven and earth, you dwell on a high and holy place and also with the contrite and lowly of spirit. I ask for the grace of true contrition, so that I would humble myself under your almighty hand and put no confidence in the flesh. Keep me from the self-deception that would make me think too highly of myself. You know all my thoughts and motives. Even my best deeds can be tainted with the selfish desire for recognition and applause. But as I learn to make you my audience instead of playing to an audience of many, there is no place for pretense or hiding or posturing. All things are open and laid bare before your eyes, and only your assessment will matter in the end. I pray in Jesus' name. Amen.

day22

MARK 4:37–41

A furious squall came up, and the waves broke over the boat, so that it was nearly swamped. Jesus was in the stern, sleeping on a cushion. The disciples woke him up and said to him, "Teacher, don't you care if we drown?"

He got up, rebuked the wind and said to the waves, "Quiet! Be still!" Then the wind died down and it was completely calm.

He said to his disciples, "Why are you so afraid? Do you still have no faith?"

They were terrified and asked each other, "Who is this? Even the wind and the waves obey him!"

READ ALSO MARK 5:1–17.

MEDITATION

Something about Jesus drew the disciples to him. But it is clear that they really had no idea who they had signed on with. A storm big enough to frighten weathered fishermen was nothing to Jesus. "Be still!" he says as someone who has spoken to the waves before, and they were.

But notice the response of his disciples. "Who is this?" they ask, because they have never seen, probably never heard of, anyone with such authority. A demon-possessed man who had been terrorizing a city falls to his knees before him, and Jesus is unmoved. "Come out!" Jesus says. The demon does, and the people are afraid and beg Jesus to leave.

There is something about that kind of power that is both attractive and repellent. Like the disciples, we sometimes fail to realize who we have signed up to follow. Like the Gerasenes, we sometimes hold Jesus off, afraid of what else he might do. We call Jesus "Savior," but we forget the staggering ramifications of the fact that he is also "Lord."

In a few verses, Mark demonstrates Jesus' lordship over natural forces (a raging sea), over the spirit world (the demon-possessed man), and, if we were to keep reading, we would see him conquer disease and death as well. If Jesus' disciples had any question about the authority of this God-man they were following, they would soon be reassured. These were not tricks. Jesus possessed all authority in heaven and on earth. And maybe the most remarkable thing about his authority is that he chose to use it to suffer and die in our place, instead of exercising that authority to save himself from death on a cross. ✤

PRAYER

Lord Jesus, you are exalted above all that I can conceive or even imagine. You created everything and have authority over everything. Time and space, disease, disaster and even death are all part of your created order—you brought them into being and you rule over them. You are the beginning and the end, the Alpha and the Omega, the First and the Last. Your matchless power knows no bounds. Yet you, in your humility, chose to restrain your powers and die for powerless and sinful people like me. I confess that I love to call you Savior, but it is often difficult for me to surrender to you as Lord. Forgive my arrogance, and help me to place the whole of my life under your sovereign rule. In your mighty name I pray. Amen.

day23

PSALM 42:1–3,9–11

As the deer pants for streams of water, so my soul pants for you, my God. My soul thirsts for God, for the living God. When can I go and meet with God? My tears have been my food day and night, while people say to me all day long, "Where is your God?" ...

I say to God my Rock, "Why have you forgotten me? Why must I go about mourning, oppressed by the enemy?" My bones suffer mortal agony as my foes taunt me, saying to me all day long, "Where is your God?" Why, my soul, are you downcast? Why so disturbed within me? Put your hope in God, for I will yet praise him, my Savior and my God.

MATTHEW 5:6

"Blessed are those who hunger and thirst for righteousness, for they will be filled."

JOHN 4:7–11,13–14

When a Samaritan woman came to draw water, Jesus said to her, "Will you give me a drink?" ...

The Samaritan woman said to him, "You are a Jew and I am a Samaritan woman. How can you ask me for a drink?" ... Jesus answered her, "If you knew the gift of God and who it is that asks you for a drink, you would have asked him and he would have given you living water."

"Sir," the woman said, "you have nothing to draw with and the well is deep. Where can you get this living water?" ...

Jesus answered, "Everyone who drinks this water will be thirsty again, but whoever drinks the water I give them will never thirst. Indeed, the water I give them will become in them a spring of water welling up to eternal life."

JOHN 7:37–38

On the last and greatest day of the festival, Jesus stood and said in a loud voice, "Let anyone who is thirsty come to me and drink. Whoever believes in me, as Scripture has said, rivers of living water will flow from within them."

JOHN 19:28

Later, knowing that everything had now been finished, and so that Scripture would be fulfilled, Jesus said, "I am thirsty."

MEDITATION

The Old Testament poets had far less knowledge about the person and promises of God than we enjoy through the fullness of New Testament revelation. Yet they seem to have had a much better grasp on what it is to thirst for God than we do. That thirst, so necessary to true discipleship, is dulled in us by worry and the desire for other things. But Jesus called that hunger and thirst for true righteousness (which can only be found in him) "blessed." It is this longing that leads us to the realization that we are meant to live for more than the things we see and strive for. This thirst leads us into a deeper relationship with Jesus and becomes a spring that overflows from us to the lives of others.

What do you want more than anything in the world? The question calls for a decision: follow hard after God or chase after everything else. One path leads to intimacy with God, the other to idolatry. For the Samaritan woman, there was no question. The future hope she desired was standing right in front of her, asking for a drink. And on the cross, as his sacrifice on our behalf is nearing completion, Jesus is like a distance runner at the finish line. He has only the strength and breath to say, "I am thirsty," and then he commits his finished work and his spirit to the Father, so that we will never have to thirst again.   ❖

PRAYER

God of grace, I live in a dry and weary land. I have tasted how good you are, and it has both satisfied me and made me thirsty for more of you. I so desperately need what only you can provide, and yet I confess that I often search in other places. I do not desire you as much as I ought to, but I want to want you more. I wish to be filled with a holy longing. Show me a glimpse of your glory, and my thirst will be quickened again. You sent your Son to pour out his life for me. Show me how I may find utter satisfaction as I pour out my life now in service to you and to others. And when I am tempted to seek satisfaction in other places, discipline me gently to bring me back to you as my only true source of strength. In Jesus' name I pray. Amen.

day24

JOHN 8:2–11

At dawn [Jesus] appeared again in the temple courts, where all the people gathered around him, and he sat down to teach them. The teachers of the law and the Pharisees brought in a woman caught in adultery. They made her stand before the group and said to Jesus, "Teacher, this woman was caught in the act of adultery. In the Law Moses commanded us to stone such women. Now what do you say?" They were using this question as a trap, in order to have a basis for accusing him.

But Jesus bent down and started to write on the ground with his finger. When they kept on questioning him, he straightened up and said to them, "Let any one of you who is without sin be the first to throw a stone at her." Again he stooped down and wrote on the ground.

At this, those who heard began to go away one at a time, the older ones first, until only Jesus was left, with the woman still standing there. Jesus straightened up and asked her, "Woman, where are they? Has no one condemned you?"

"No one, sir," she said.

"Then neither do I condemn you," Jesus declared. "Go now and leave your life of sin."

MATTHEW 9:13

"But go and learn what this means: 'I desire mercy, not sacrifice.' For I have not come to call the righteous, but sinners."

JOHN 3:17

For God did not send his Son into the world to condemn the world, but to save the world through him.

READ ALSO 1 CORINTHIANS 6:9–11 AND COLOSSIANS 1:21–22.

MEDITATION

Jesus saw our accuser face to face. For 40 days, hungry and exhausted, he withstood the devil's temptations and misrepresentations. "*If* you are the Son of God, then ..." Jesus never bought into the lie that he might not be who God said he was. He persisted. Accusation (false or true) is one of the enemy's favorite tactics.

And in this passage (see John 8:2–11), when challenged to rule on the charges against this woman who they said was guilty of breaking the law, Jesus called to mind a higher law, one revealed through the prophet Hosea, one he had already advised these men to contemplate: "I desire mercy, not sacrifice." Sacrifices were religious offerings to God that were often bloody, requiring violence. Mercy, on the other hand, was represented by gentleness and kindness and was a sign of the heart, not merely an act of religion. So Jesus bent down in the dirt long enough to distract the gaze of these men from the woman, long enough for her to regain her composure, wrap herself in something. And then Jesus said something that caused her accusers to walk away, one by one, just as his accuser, thwarted, had left him in the wilderness. Jesus had not come to condemn the immoral; he had come to rescue them. He had come to gather those who were far off and filthy and wash them clean, to show them mercy and present them to the Father, free from all accusation.   ❖

PRAYER

Heavenly Father, you are the rescuer and deliverer of my soul. Through your Son, you stooped down in order to lift me up. I was dead in my sins and trespasses. I was held captive in the snare of the devil to do his will, but Jesus came to overthrow this bondage and to liberate me, to call me his beloved. You have granted me the glorious gift of acceptance and welcome in Christ. Through the powerful work of the Savior, I am rescued from the domain of darkness and transferred into your kingdom, without fault, without blemish. And you will not hear an accusation against me again. Just as you have accepted and forgiven me, may I also accept and forgive those who have sinned against me. Rather than despising those who have done wrong, may I reach out to them with your healing love and mercy. In Christ's name I pray. Amen.

day25

JOHN 1:1,14

In the beginning was the Word, and the Word was with God, and the Word was God ... The Word became flesh and made his dwelling among us. We have seen his glory, the glory of the one and only Son, who came from the Father, full of grace and truth.

ISAIAH 53:2–3

He grew up before him like a tender shoot, and like a root out of dry ground. He had no beauty or majesty to attract us to him, nothing in his appearance that we should desire him. He was despised and rejected by mankind, a man of suffering, and familiar with pain. Like one from whom people hide their faces he was despised, and we held him in low esteem.

JOHN 17:1,4–5

After Jesus said this, he looked toward heaven and prayed: "Father, the hour has come. Glorify your Son, that your Son may glorify you ... I have brought you glory on earth by finishing the work you gave me to do. And now, Father, glorify me in your presence with the glory I had with you before the world began."

READ ALSO HEBREWS 12:1–2, 2 PETER 1:16 AND 1 CORINTHIANS 1:27–28.

MEDITATION

It is nearly Easter, and we will hang crosses on the walls of our homes and churches. How do we think of it when it's a decoration? With all of our present-day associations with the cross — an object of Christian identification and adoration — it is almost impossible to see the cross for what it actually was. And when we fail to understand the cross, we fail to properly understand what our Lord suffered on our behalf: shame.

Jesus despised the cross. To even speak of the cross in his time was disgusting. It was a punishment reserved for the worst of the nation's criminals. It was designed to bring about the utmost torture to lawbreakers.

So to say that Jesus "endured the cross, scorning its shame," is not to say "poor Jesus." It is to say that Jesus loved us so much and was so submitted to the Father that he not only endured torment, but also public humiliation. And when it was over, he was exalted to the highest place of dignity and honor in the universe. ❖

PRAYER

Jesus, Lord of glory, you came to earth and took the form of a servant and willingly suffered an unimaginable death on the cross. You died for me, a sinner. You paid the penalty for my sins. Such amazing love is utterly incomprehensible to me. Help me to understand that the path to glory often requires a sojourn through difficulties and challenges, but that you are always with me. I seek to follow you in all my ways. I know that serving you is true freedom. In your name I pray. Amen.

day26

JOHN 13:12–17

When he had finished washing their feet, he put on his clothes and returned to his place. "Do you understand what I have done for you?" he asked them. "You call me 'Teacher' and 'Lord,' and rightly so, for that is what I am. Now that I, your Lord and Teacher, have washed your feet, you also should wash one another's feet. I have set you an example that you should do as I have done for you. Very truly I tell you, no servant is greater than his master, nor is a messenger greater than the one who sent him. Now that you know these things, you will be blessed if you do them."

MEDITATION

Jesus of Nazareth had gained quite a following. People were looking for him to do something great, lead an uprising, fight for a new kingdom, a new position, more power. But he rejected the popular idea of greatness in order to introduce God's idea of it. No one, before or since, has ever embodied this virtue better than Jesus did, and there is no time he more clearly modeled it than on the night before his crucifixion.

The disciples got into a little scuffle after dinner about which one of them was the greatest (see Luke 22:24). Apparently, the lesson Jesus had doled out to the Pharisees six months before about sitting in the lowest position, rather than elbowing their way to the top, had been forgotten (see Luke 14:7–11). Luke gives us a straightforward account of Jesus' verbal response to those disciples: "For all those who exalt themselves will be humbled, and those who humble themselves will be exalted" (v. 11). But here we have his visual response, a parable about service, performed by the greatest man who ever lived. When no servant was available to wash their feet, Jesus assumed the role. The Master became the servant. The Most High got down on his knees. Jesus horrified his disciples by demonstrating to them the divine perspective, which turned their entire social order upside down. And then he commanded them to do the same. In one stunning act, Jesus demonstrated that, in the kingdom of God, service is not the path to greatness; service is greatness.   ❖

PRAYER

Lord God, just as your beloved Son came into the world to serve others and not to be served, I too want to be a servant. The more I grasp my true identity and the dignity of my position as your beloved child, the more free I become to serve others, even when they do not reciprocate, and the less I am in the bondage of being defined by the opinions and expectations others have of me. I want you to define me so I can be liberated. I want to know who I am in Christ so I have nothing to prove. I invite your Holy Spirit to make it possible for me to live an other-centered lifestyle. Teach me how to develop a vision for what you are doing in the lives of others, and give me the joy of helping them mature and reach their potential. In Christ's name I pray. Amen.

day27

ZECHARIAH 9:9

Rejoice greatly, Daughter Zion! Shout, Daughter Jerusalem! See, your king comes to you, righteous and victorious, lowly and riding on a donkey, on a colt, the foal of a donkey.

LUKE 19:32–38

Those who were sent ahead went and found it just as he had told them. As they were untying the colt, its owners asked them, "Why are you untying the colt?"

They replied, "The Lord needs it."

They brought it to Jesus, threw their cloaks on the colt and put Jesus on it. As he went along, people spread their cloaks on the road.

When he came near the place where the road goes down the Mount of Olives, the whole crowd of disciples began joyfully to praise God in loud voices for all the miracles they had seen:

"Blessed is the king who comes in the name of the Lord!"

"Peace in heaven and glory in the highest!"

READ ALSO MATTHEW 21:4–5 AND LUKE 19:29–31.

MEDITATION

The Gospels never record Jesus riding anything until now; he walked everywhere. So it seems that this day, he is making a point: He really is the Messiah that Zechariah had promised. It is a little humorous to think of him on this tiny animal—not a donkey (the sign of a king who comes in peace), but a donkey's foal. Jesus uses the most extreme example he can to show people how serious he is about fulfilling this prophecy.

But, like so many of us, the people see what they want to see. They cheer, but what they are cheering is not the real Messiah. They are hailing a king they hope will set them free from Roman oppression. They hail him with date palm branches that signify Jewish nationalism. They try to hang on him their own political aspirations.

Sound familiar? Even if you had not read this story, you might be able to guess what happens next. What always happens when we try to make God accomplish our aspirations? He refuses. Jesus rides his donkey through the eastern entrance to Jerusalem, heading straight toward the temple, and then does nothing. And when Jesus failed to do what they wanted him to do, they turned on him. And soon, instead of singing, "Blessed is the king!" they shouted, "Crucify!" To them, it was blasphemy for this man who would not fulfill their desires to be called king. And so he went to the cross, not defeated, but to do exactly as he had planned all along.   ♣

PRAYER

Lord of glory and wisdom, your sovereign plans and purposes cannot be thwarted by our sinful choices. You have revealed to me everything I need to grow in intimacy with you. I ask that the choices I make would be in conformity with your will. Please guide my actions so that I will honor your name by accomplishing your will for me. I look to you to order my steps. In Jesus' holy name I pray. Amen.

day28

JEREMIAH 31:31,33

"The days are coming," declares the LORD, "when I will make a new covenant with the people of Israel and with the people of Judah ... I will put my law in their minds and write it on their hearts. I will be their God, and they will be my people."

MATTHEW 26:27–28

Then he took a cup, and when he had given thanks, he gave it to them, saying, "Drink from it, all of you. This is my blood of the covenant, which is poured out for many for the forgiveness of sins."

ACTS 2:41–42

Those who accepted [Peter's] message were baptized, and about three thousand were added to their number that day.

They devoted themselves to the apostles' teaching and to fellowship, to the breaking of bread and to prayer.

READ ALSO EZEKIEL 36:26–27, LUKE 22:19 AND 1 CORINTHIANS 11:26.

MEDITATION

God did not give the Israelites the Ten Commandments so they would obey and be saved. He gave them the law so they would know how to live as his people. But God knew they would not be able to keep the law. He knew his people had a sin nature that would inevitably override their desire to be obedient. In fact, it was always his plan to use the law to tutor them along, restraining them externally until the time was right. Then God would do something really astonishing. He would put his Spirit inside of his people, and they would begin being transformed from within.

But there was much debate over when that day would come. When would this new covenant take effect? What were the conditions necessary for God to implement the fullness of his plan? That pathway to life for all people required the death of the Son of God. And so it was that Jesus, on the night he was betrayed, took up two simple elements: bread and wine. He blessed them and distributed them to his friends, saying, "The time has come. The new covenant will be ratified by my blood and my blood alone." The bread would represent his broken body, and the wine is his blood. He did it all. Our task is to remember, and as often as we do this, we proclaim the benefits of his death until his return. ✣

PRAYER

Lord God, by the power of your Holy Spirit at work within me, teach me to desire you more than anything else, to do what you command, to hope in your promises, to trust in you and to wait for your timing in all things. I confess that it is often easy to overlook the voice of your Spirit in the noise and bustle of this world. Thank you for this new covenant. Thank you for the gift of the Holy Spirit to guide me and comfort me. May I walk in utter dependence on his counsel. In Christ's name I pray. Amen.

day29

MATTHEW 26:36–39

Then Jesus went with his disciples to a place called Gethsemane, and he said to them, "Sit here while I go over there and pray." He took Peter and the two sons of Zebedee along with him, and he began to be sorrowful and troubled. Then he said to them, "My soul is overwhelmed with sorrow to the point of death. Stay here and keep watch with me." Going a little farther, he fell with his face to the ground and prayed, "My father, if it is possible, may this cup be taken from me. Yet not as I will, but as you will."

LUKE 22:43–44

An angel from heaven appeared to him and strengthened him. And being in anguish, he prayed more earnestly, and his sweat was like drops of blood falling to the ground.

MATTHEW 26:40–46

Then he returned to his disciples and found them sleeping. "Couldn't you men keep watch with me for one hour?" he asked Peter. "Watch and pray so that you will not fall into temptation. The spirit is willing, but the flesh is weak." He went away a second time and prayed, "My father, if it is not possible for this cup to be taken away unless I drink it, may your will be done." When he came back, he again found them sleeping, because their eyes were heavy. So he left them and went away once more and prayed a third time, saying the same thing. Then he returned to the disciples and said to them, "Are you still sleeping and resting? Look, the hour has come, and the Son of Man is delivered into the hands of sinners. Rise! Let us go! Here comes my betrayer!"

HEBREWS 5:7–9

During the days of Jesus' life on earth, he offered up prayers and petitions with fervent cries and tears to the one who could save him from death, and he was heard because of his reverent submission. Son though he was, he learned obedience from what he suffered and, once made perfect, he became the source of eternal salvation for all who obey him.

MEDITATION

Jesus said, "Keep watch with me." If you have ever sat with a loved one while waiting for that person to die, perhaps you know something of how the three men who waited with Jesus might have felt. He had told them, repeatedly, that he was going away. But now they see him in anguish, and they can see that it is all starting to happen, in perhaps a more terrible way than they had imagined. They could not understand what would come in the next few days, so the waiting was full of dread, the dark kind of sadness that feels unbearable.

Jesus said, "My soul is overwhelmed to the point of death. Stay here and keep watch with me." But instead they fell asleep. Still, if we disparage the disciples for their inability to stay awake, maybe we haven't spent enough time thinking about this scene, and maybe we have never prayed to the point of exhaustion. There is a point at which our circumstances can no longer be examined. There is a point after which a person can pray no more. This is when the Holy Spirit must take over for us "through wordless groans" (Romans 8:26), perhaps even while we sleep.

Jesus asked God three times to take away the suffering that was coming, not just the torture and ridicule, but the unbearable thought of facing all of God's wrath at once, the Father's hatred for sin all falling at once on the head of his innocent Son. But Jesus followed his request with "may your will be done."

When we ask God for something three times, and he does not give us what we want, we are often angry and begin to question his goodness. And when our friends fail us, we may want to find new friends. But Jesus, even as he faced the beginning of the most terrible time there ever was on earth, went back to encourage the friends who had failed him and to face his mission before God: the price of our salvation.   ❖

PRAYER

Loving Father, I gripe and grumble when I encounter painful circumstances. I complain about bad luck or not getting the breaks in life. I wonder why you allow such pain to occur to me and to others. Yet I know that I can take my grievances directly and openly to you. I can admit my confusion and my disappointment. I know I am approaching the only One who can really do something in my times of need. Thank you for your patience and your kindness to me. In Jesus' name I pray. Amen.

day30

JOHN 11:47–50,53

Then the chief priests and the Pharisees called a meeting of the Sanhedrin.

"What are we accomplishing?" they asked. "Here is this man performing many signs. If we let him go on like this, everyone will believe in him, and then the Romans will come and take away both our temple and our nation." Then one of them, named Caiaphas, who was high priest that year, spoke up, "You know nothing at all! You do not realize that it is better for you that one man die for the people than that the whole nation perish" …

So from that day on they plotted to take his life.

JOHN 18:1–3

When he had finished praying, Jesus left with his disciples and crossed the Kidron Valley. On the other side there was a garden, and he and his disciples went into it. Now Judas, who betrayed him, knew the place, because Jesus had often met there with his disciples. So Judas came to the garden, guiding a detachment of soldiers and some officials from the chief priests and the Pharisees. They were carrying torches, lanterns and weapons.

JOHN 18:12–14

Then the detachment of soldiers with its commander and the Jewish officials arrested Jesus. They bound him and brought him first to Annas, who was the father-in-law of Caiaphas, the high priest that year. Caiaphas was the one who had advised the Jewish leaders that it would be good if one man died for the people.

LUKE 22:66–71

At daybreak the council of the elders of the people, both the chief priests and the teachers of the law, met together, and Jesus was led before them. "If you are the Messiah," they said, "tell us." Jesus answered, "If I tell you, you will not believe me, and if I asked you, you would not answer. But from now on, the Son of Man will be seated at the right hand of the mighty God." They all asked, "Are you then the Son of God?" He replied, "You say that I am." Then they said, "Why do we need any more testimony? We have heard it from his own lips."

MEDITATION

Jesus, the only person to never sin, the most loving and perfect human to ever walk the earth, surrendered himself into the hands of these men, knowing they would execute him. He could have saved himself. He could have walked away (he'd done that before when a group attempted to stone him). He could have called angels from heaven to wage holy war against his enemies. But he did not. He did nothing to save himself because he was submitting to the will of the Father.

God's justice says sin must be punished. A debt has been incurred and restitution must be made. Jesus was well aware of this, having spoken about hell more than he did about heaven, and he was determined that no one need go there. He knew that only a sinless sacrifice could atone for the sins of every human being in the world—one sacrifice for all. He knew this was all part of God's plan to ultimately triumph over evil. And so, because of his faith in his Father's perfect plan, the Son suffered on the cross the condemnation that we deserve but never have to experience. The apostle Paul would later write, "Therefore, there is now no condemnation for those who are in Christ Jesus" (Romans 8:1). The price has been paid in full. Let us remain in Christ and praise him for having chosen to suffer in our place. ✤

PRAYER

Lord Jesus, because of your love, you were obedient to your Father's will, even to the point of taking my sin and my shame onto yourself in an agonizing death on the cross. You willingly embraced the purpose for which you came to earth. You knew that this was the only way to lead others into freedom and eternal life. May I learn to look beyond the immediate pains of this life to see what you are preparing for me. May I learn that it is through giving up my life for your sake that I will truly find the life that is abundant and blessed. May I learn the wisdom of humbling myself now so that I will later be exalted. In your precious name I pray. Amen.

day31

PSALM 41:9

Even my close friend, someone I trusted, one who shared my bread, has turned against me.

MARK 14:43

Just as he was speaking, Judas, one of the Twelve, appeared. With him was a crowd armed with swords and clubs, sent from the chief priests, the teachers of the law, and the elders.

MARK 14:44–46

Now the betrayer had arranged a signal with them: "The one I kiss is the man; arrest him and lead him away under guard." Going at once to Jesus, Judas said, "Rabbi!" and kissed him. The men seized Jesus and arrested him.

MARK 14:50

Then everyone deserted him and fled.

READ ALSO JOHN 18:4–10, LUKE 22:51, MATTHEW 26:52–54 AND LUKE 22:52–53.

MEDITATION

Betrayal is an agony like no other. There are no wounds quite as devastating as those inflicted by someone we thought was a trusted friend. Jesus knew this pain. His close friend, whom he taught and loved and shared meals with for years, sold him out for 30 silver coins. And yet Jesus shows us that even this pain can be redeemed; because of his experience, he shows us that none of us has to suffer through betrayal alone. He walks that path with us.

Pain does not necessarily lead to growth in character. Improperly processed, pain can lead us to bitterness and destruction. But Jesus demonstrates that we can choose to use our pain to purchase empathy and compassion for others.

How did Jesus deal with betrayal? He remained steadfast. He remained true to his identity, and he refused to exact revenge or even to defend himself. The same will be true for you. When you are betrayed, there may be nothing left but to commit yourself to God and know that you are not alone. Pray that the character being cultivated in you and the glory you will one day see will far outweigh the pain of the moment.   ✤

PRAYER

God of redemptive grace, you have given me the astonishing gift of being reconciled to you through my faith in the person and work of Jesus Christ. You have overcome my enmity and given me the gift of peace with you now and the hope of glory throughout all of eternity. Still, you have also said that in this world I will encounter hardship and pain. Remind me that I can bring all my sorrow to you, because you sent your Son to suffer for me. Never let me forget that my experience of betrayal and pain will be brief in light of eternity, and that you are perfecting, confirming, strengthening and establishing me in Christ. Amen.

day32

ISAIAH 9:7

Of the greatness of his government and peace there will be no end. He will reign on David's throne and over his kingdom, establishing and upholding it with justice and righteousness from that time on and forever. The zeal of the LORD Almighty will accomplish this.

1 PETER 2:22

"He committed no sin, and no deceit was found in his mouth."

HEBREWS 4:15

For we do not have a high priest who is unable to empathize with our weaknesses, but we have one who has been tempted in every way, just as we are—yet he did not sin.

READ ALSO HEBREWS 13:8 AND ALL OF MATTHEW 26.

MEDITATION

The Son of David, who was to come and deliver his people, would be just and righteous and zealous for God. We would say he had integrity. And he did. Jesus' love, his truth and his goodness were not governed by external circumstances or personal ambitions, but were always steadfastly in accordance with the will of the Father.

Here is our Lord Jesus, standing in stark contrast before a man who is the exact opposite of integrity—a hypocrite. Caiaphas models everything Jesus is not—a manipulator too busy with his own selfish plans to mediate for the sins of the people. He had set this whole scene up, proposing that Jesus be killed so that Rome would not take away his job—and his status. It was Caiaphas who had suggested that one man should be sacrificed for the nation (John 11:45–53).

But we have to stop and think: Here is the high priest of the Jewish nation, essentially making a sacrifice to Rome to keep what he does not want to lose. So when Jesus stands before him and does not deny his own divinity, Caiaphas plays out a response he probably has rehearsed, pretending to be terribly upset. Jesus is silent; a man of integrity knows better than to argue with an actor. Jesus knew that Caiaphas had made up his mind long before this trial ever began. In light of this story, we have a choice: to follow Caiaphas and love what we have so much that we will lie, cheat and kill to keep it, or to lay down our lives and follow the one who modeled integrity and is, himself, our righteousness.   ❖

PRAYER

God of glory, you want what is best for me. Yet, I attempt to control my own life, and I sabotage the peace and joy that come from submitting to your will. Help me to remember that it is in the small decisions of life that my character is forged. Small acts of hypocrisy always lead to larger acts of infidelity. Give me the wisdom and humility to seek accountability and honesty with a few people, so that they can protect me from myself. Keep me from being hardened by the deceitfulness of sin. In your Son's name I pray. Amen.

day33

ISAIAH 53:7–8

He was oppressed and afflicted, yet he did not open his mouth … By oppression and judgment he was taken away … For he was cut off from the land of the living; for the transgression of my people he was punished.

1 JOHN 2:1

My dear children, I write this to you so that you will not sin. But if anybody does sin, we have an advocate with the Father—Jesus Christ, the Righteous One.

HEBREWS 7:25

He is able to save completely those who come to God through him, because he always lives to intercede for them.

READ ALSO MATTHEW 27:1–14.

MEDITATION

We have all heard about Jesus' trials, the false accusations, his refusal to defend himself, the problem over jurisdiction because no one wanted to take responsibility for what the mob wanted to see done to him. At every step of the proceedings, Jesus' accusers were making their preposterous case. But where was Jesus' defense counsel? There was none.

In Jesus' time, it would have been Pilate's responsibility to ensure a fair trial, but Pilate was a coward and refused to stand up to the rabid crowd. So Jesus stood trial alone. Since he was our substitute, this was right. There was no need to plead his innocence, because, ultimately, he was on trial for our sins, and we are all guilty.

But unlike Jesus, we will never stand trial alone against the debilitating, demeaning and destructive power of sin. Today, the One who had no legal counsel stands and advocates for us—always. Every time the accuser comes before God to condemn us, Jesus defends us, not by claiming our innocence, but by pleading the ongoing effects of his own death. And, so that we will not forget this important fact, he sends his Holy Spirit (*paracletos* in Greek, meaning "called alongside") to stand beside us, just as legal counsel does in court. Jesus stood alone so we will never have to. Every time we sin, Jesus is there, standing with us, as a perpetual reminder to the court that the case is closed. And because we are so loved, our Advocate will always be heard.   ❖

PRAYER

Lord Jesus, through your powerful work, I have been rescued from the domain of darkness and transferred into your kingdom. In spite of my guilt, you reached out to me and lifted me out of the abyss. In my desperate need, you showed me grace. I recognized my condition and responded to your loving call through faith. You declared me righteous and reconciled me to my Creator. I now enjoy peace and joy that I would have not known otherwise. Help me to avoid sin. And remind me that when I do fail you, you stand as my Advocate and Defender. In your righteous name I pray. Amen.

day34

MARK 15:12–14

"What shall I do then, with the one you call the king of the Jews?" Pilate asked them. "Crucify him!" they shouted. "Why? What crime has he committed?" asked Pilate. But they shouted all the louder, "Crucify him!"

READ ALSO JOHN 18:28–40.

MEDITATION

It always comes as a shock when religious leaders fail to act in godly ways. But it has always been thus. We must remember that religious leaders are just mortals. We are all susceptible to sin. We all make poor choices. We all, from time to time, put our own interests first. And so it should come as no surprise when religious leaders fail to use their power wisely.

The religious leaders of Jesus' day were an extreme example of this. They were so concerned about being defiled by entering a Gentile residence that they would not enter the palace. Yet they had just come from an illegal trial after plotting the murder of an innocent man. Envy drove them to murder Jesus. They feared the loss of power and went to this extreme to keep it.

Pilate knew that truth was being ignored. He did not know that he was staring truth in the face, for he, like the ones outside his door shouting, "Crucify him!" was blinded by the pursuit of his own agenda. The ability to do something we know is wrong and then to justify it shows the power of the flesh, the power of self-deception. Envy and seeking our own power will always kill the Christ in us and blind us to the truth. Pray that we are not too much like those religious leaders. Pray that we do not miss our chance to see truth and honor it. ♣

PRAYER

Lord Jesus, you are truth. You bring life, hope, purpose, fulfillment and power to all who will submit to your authority. You fulfill all the Messianic prophecies. Your redeeming work earns you the title of Savior of the World. You will certainly come to judge the world and rule in righteousness. Until then, I want to be a herald of your kingdom, which will one day come in its fullness. I know I can only accomplish this as I submit to your lordship. I want to be an agent of positive change in this world by obeying your commands and walking in your power. The values of your kingdom appear so upside-down to those whose eyes have grown accustomed to this world. You teach that we all are to be servants, that the last will be first, the humble will be exalted, the giver will receive and the poor in spirit will be rich. Open my eyes this day to see you. I ask this in the power of your name. Amen.

day35

LUKE 23:4–12

Pilate announced to the chief priests and the crowd, "I find no basis for a charge against this man."

But they insisted, "He stirs up the people all over Judea by his teaching. He started in Galilee and has come all the way here."

On hearing this, Pilate asked if the man was a Galilean. When he learned that Jesus was under Herod's jurisdiction, he sent him to Herod, who was also in Jerusalem at that time.

When Herod saw Jesus, he was greatly pleased, because for a long time he had been wanting to see him. From what he had heard about him, he hoped to see him perform a sign of some sort. He plied him with many questions, but Jesus gave him no answer. The chief priests and the teachers of the law were standing there, vehemently accusing him. Then Herod and his soldiers ridiculed and mocked him. Dressing him in an elegant robe, they sent him back to Pilate. That day Herod and Pilate became friends—before this they had been enemies.

MATTHEW 12:38–41

Then some of the Pharisees and teachers of the law said to him, "Teacher, we want to see a sign from you."

He answered, "A wicked and adulterous generation asks for a sign! But none will be given it except the sign of the prophet Jonah. For as Jonah was three days and three nights in the belly of a huge fish, so the Son of Man will be three days and three nights in the heart of the earth. The men of Nineveh will stand up at the judgment with this generation and condemn it; for they repented at the preaching of Jonah, and now something greater than Jonah is here."

LUKE 16:29–31

"Abraham replied, 'They have Moses and the Prophets; let them listen to them.'

"'No, father Abraham,' he said, 'but if someone from the dead goes to them, they will repent.'

"He said to him, 'If they do not listen to Moses and the Prophets, they will not be convinced even if someone rises from the dead.'"

MEDITATION

Herod had power. It was limited by the Romans, but it was there. He knew what it felt like to wave his hand or utter a word and see his will done. Powerful men are often fascinated by other powerful men, and Herod had heard all about Jesus' astonishing abilities. It had been said that Jesus could heal sick people, feed large crowds, even walk on water. So Herod was actually excited to see Jesus. He wanted nothing more than to see Jesus perform one of those magic tricks. But Jesus disappoints him. He refuses to play along.

This is something we do not readily admit very often: He does the same with us. Jesus is many things: Loving. Wise. Patient. Humble. The perfect embodiment of both grace and truth. And, if we are honest, we are forced to add that Jesus is frustrating. He refuses to cooperate with our plans for him. He has his own agenda, and he will not be swayed from it. Of course, if Herod had just waited, he would have received the greatest sign imaginable. In three days, Jesus would come back to life. But that was not the kind of sign Herod wanted. He wanted a coin trick or a card trick or something amusing. He did not want something that might actually have implications for how he ought to live. Strange as it seems, Herod was probably in town when Jesus came out of the tomb. But he was not convinced, even though Jesus rose from the dead. Some people are like that. Hard to convince.   ♣

PRAYER

Loving Savior, I live in a time of doubt and skepticism. But the Gospels proclaim the many amazing things you did in your lifetime. You demonstrated your authority over nature, over demons, over disease. And then you conquered death. But you did all of this on your own timetable, refusing to be manipulated by people. You never bent to our agenda. Instead, you ask us to bend to yours. Teach me to look beyond what you may be able to do for me and see you for who you are. Show me the wisdom of seeking your face and the joy of knowing your presence. And remind me that the greatest sign of all is not a little more food or the calming of a storm but the promise of life beyond the grave, reveling through all of eternity with you. In your strong and mighty name I pray. Amen.

day36

LUKE 22:31–34

"Simon, Simon, Satan has asked to sift all of you as wheat. But I have prayed for you, Simon, that your faith may not fail. And when you have turned back, strengthen your brothers." But he replied, "Lord, I am ready to go with you to prison and to death." Jesus answered, "I tell you, Peter, before the rooster crows today, you will deny three times that you know me."

JOHN 18:15–18

Simon Peter and another disciple were following Jesus [after his arrest]. Because this disciple was known to the high priest, he went with Jesus into the high priest's courtyard, but Peter had to wait outside at the door. The other disciple, who was known to the high priest, came back, spoke to the servant girl on duty there and brought Peter in. "You aren't one of this man's disciples too, are you?" she asked Peter. He replied, "I am not." It was cold, and the servants and officials stood around a fire they had made to keep warm. Peter also was standing with them, warming himself.

MATTHEW 26:71–73

Then he went out to the gateway, where another servant girl saw him and said to the people there, "This fellow was with Jesus of Nazareth." He denied it again, with an oath: "I don't know the man!" After a little while, those standing there went up to Peter and said, "Surely you are one of them; your accent gives you away."

JOHN 18:26

One of the high priest's servants, a relative of the man whose ear Peter had cut off, challenged him, "Didn't I see you with him in the garden?"

MATTHEW 26:74–75

Then he began to call down curses, and he swore to them, "I don't know the man!" Immediately a rooster crowed. Then Peter remembered the word Jesus had spoken: "Before the rooster crows, you will disown me three times." And he went outside and wept bitterly.

MEDITATION

The Bible doesn't whitewash over character faults. Peter failed miserably, and it's all there in black and white for us to read. Under intense pressure, he abandoned his master and friend in his hour of trial. He failed him in the garden. When Jesus asked him to watch and pray, Peter fell asleep. Now he denied knowing the One he said he would follow to prison, even if it meant death, not once but three times. And so he weeps. Bitterly. He feels his failure, and it breaks him. But this is not a story about Peter. This is a story about Jesus, and Jesus knew this would happen—probably even before he chose Peter. He knew how Peter would be shaken, sifted by Satan until his most sinful inclinations surfaced and could be exploited. And he knew that Peter would be made perfect through such suffering. This would, in the end, be used for good in Peter's life. Something would be forged in him that would not be there otherwise. God always redeems what he allows, even our worst failures — perhaps especially our worst failures. It is through these failures that our pride and self-reliance lose their grip on our souls, and we are set free to run into the future God has for us. ❖

PRAYER

Lord, you know me better than I know myself. You know what I am capable of. You know my limitations. You know my intentions, and you know that, while my spirit is often willing, my flesh is often so very weak. And yet you chose me anyway. Your love amazes me. I want to immerse myself in you completely so that Satan cannot use me. I know that your ultimate destiny for me is that I become conformed to your image. Rid me of my self-reliance. Break the spine of my pride. Teach me the blessings of finding my sense of identity and worth only in you. And when I fail you, gently restore me, using even my failures to your greater glory. In Jesus' name I pray. Amen.

day37

ROMANS 6:23

For the wages of sin is death, but the gift of God is eternal life in Christ Jesus our Lord.

ROMANS 8:1–4

Therefore, there is now no condemnation for those who are in Christ Jesus, because through Christ Jesus the law of the Spirit who gives life has set you free from the law of sin and death. For what the law was powerless to do because it was weakened by the flesh, God did by sending his own Son in the likeness of sinful flesh to be a sin offering. And so he condemned sin in the flesh, in order that the righteous requirement of the law might be fully met in us, who do not live according to the flesh but according to the Spirit.

READ ALSO LUKE 23:32–43.

MEDITATION

What kind of man uses his dying breath to spew venom and hatred at a complete stranger? The kind of man the Romans saw fit to crucify. He could not even be trusted as a slave anymore. They felt the only recourse for such a man was public execution in the most torturous manner they could conceive. Meet the thief on the cross—not the one we normally talk about—the other one—the one writhing in agony and still joining with the crowd in heaping insults on an innocent man.

Only after surveying this character should we allow our gaze to drift to the other — the one on Jesus' other side — the one who knows he has brought this all on himself. The one who is not raging but feels the sting of shame and humiliation this punishment is intended to evoke. Now think of the courage it takes for him to take one last shot, make one last attempt at redemption. He uses his last bit of strength to come to the defense of an obviously innocent man. And then, because he knows his end is near, he makes one last request — not for deliverance from death but for something positive on the other side of it. And now allow your eyes to move to the One in the middle and realize this: As he is dying, Jesus looks with compassion on this thief to his side and grants his request. Jesus Christ grants him salvation. ✤

PRAYER

Jesus, I am so grateful for the great love and grace and mercy that you have shown to me even though I have been disobedient and rebellious. It is impossible for my mind to grasp the breadth and length and height and depth of your love. It passes all understanding. If you gave me the justice I deserve, I would have no hope. I would be alienated and estranged from you and suffer the consequences of your holy judgment. But you would not leave me in that state, choosing to offer me a grace I do not deserve. You met the righteous requirement of justice through your redemptive sacrifice on the cross. You set me free from the consequences and threw my offenses into the deepest sea. For this I praise you and offer my life as a living sacrifice for your glory. Amen.

day38

LUKE 23:44–45

It was now about noon, and darkness came over the whole land until three in the afternoon, for the sun stopped shining.

MATTHEW 27:50–54

And when Jesus had cried out again in a loud voice, he gave up his spirit.

At that moment the curtain of the temple was torn in two from top to bottom. The earth shook, the rocks split and the tombs broke open. The bodies of many holy people who had died were raised to life. They came out of the tombs after Jesus' resurrection and went into the holy city and appeared to many people.

When the centurion and those with him who were guarding Jesus saw the earthquake and all that had happened, they were terrified, and exclaimed, "Surely he was the Son of God!"

LUKE 23:48–49

When all the people who had gathered to witness this sight saw what took place, they beat their breasts and went away. But all those who knew him, including the women who had followed him from Galilee, stood at a distance, watching these things.

ROMANS 3:21–26

But now apart from the law the righteousness of

God has been made known, to which the Law and the Prophets testify. This righteousness is given through faith in Jesus Christ to all who believe. There is no difference between Jew and Gentile, for all have sinned and fall short of the glory of God, and all are justified freely by his grace through the redemption that came by Christ Jesus. God presented Christ as a sacrifice of atonement, through the shedding of his blood — to be received by faith. He did this to demonstrate his righteousness, because in his forbearance he had left the sins committed beforehand unpunished — he did it to demonstrate his righteousness at the present time, so as to be just and the one who justifies those who have faith in Jesus.

HEBREWS 9:15

For this reason Christ is the mediator of a new covenant, that those who are called may receive the promised eternal inheritance — now that he has died as a ransom to set them free from the sins committed under the first covenant.

MEDITATION

It is Good Friday. And there are a lot of good things about it. Rain falls at this time of year, sun shines and beautiful things grow. So what draws us today to think about an instrument of death? Is there not something better we could do with our day to enrich our lives? Everything in the world (especially if we are engaging in some sort of media) tells us that there are other things we could be doing to enhance our longevity, improve our lifestyle, increase our happiness.

But the truth is, there comes a time in everyone's life when we become painfully aware that these things do not bring what they promise. We are all dying to live, but the allure of this life is always proven to be an illusion, one that either ebbs away or is ripped from our hands. Our health is compromised. A relationship fails. A loved one dies. The opportunity of a lifetime falls through. People betray us. And all of a sudden, the life we worked so hard to create is suddenly much less than we had hoped for.

The truth is, what draws us to the cross and to Jesus is something deep inside us that tells us that everything that Jesus said was true. We were meant to live for more than the things of this world, and the real currency that purchased our freedom is death—Jesus' death on the cross. None of our achievements matter in light of what Jesus achieved on the day he died. Ironically, through his death he provides us with the life we have always wanted but can never attain on our own.   ✤

PRAYER

Dear God, if your abundant life were possible through human efforts, Jesus would not have had to die. I know that without him, I am incapable of truly living the life for which you created me. I cannot achieve perfection on my own. I have fallen short of your goodness, your glory and your standards. My sin separates me from you, and I am in a desperate condition without the mercy and grace I find only in the cross of your Son, my Savior, Jesus Christ. Because I trust in Jesus, he gives me what I both need and want most: the gift of eternal life with you. In his name I pray. Amen.

day39

MARK 15:43–45

Joseph of Arimathea, a prominent member of the Council, who was himself waiting for the kingdom of God, went boldly to Pilate and asked for Jesus' body. Pilate was surprised to hear that he was already dead. Summoning the centurion, he asked him if Jesus had already died. When he learned from the centurion that it was so, he gave the body to Joseph.

READ ALSO JOHN 19:31–42.

MEDITATION

Tomorrow is Easter, and we are probably, in our minds, pushing past today and thinking of the grand celebration that will take place commemorating the resurrection of Jesus. But wait. Not so fast. We would do well to remember that the people we read about in the Bible had to live this all one verse at a time. They didn't know the end of the story. They couldn't skip ahead to the next chapter. For them, this was Saturday. Jesus was dead and buried. The tomb was sealed shut. Hope was gone, lying there silently in that cave.

Why should we bother thinking about Jesus' final moments on the cross and who buried him? One answer is that there would be several false accounts that would crop up over the next several centuries, accounts which deny either the death or the resurrection of Jesus. It is essential to our faith that we know for certain that Jesus was really dead. That is why they buried him. These were not overly superstitious people; they knew when someone was dead, and they knew what to do with a dead body. You bury it. Joseph and Nicodemus go to great personal trouble and expense to honor Jesus. Though they did not stand for him in life, they now stand for him in death, preparing his body in haste so as to get him in the tomb before sundown. They intended to go back later and remove his bones. They never did. And everyone now knows why.   ❖

PRAYER

Lord Jesus, your death and resurrection form the very foundation of my faith, the source of my hope and purpose, the wellspring of my salvation, the assurance of my peace and the basis for my eternal life with you. I confess that I am often so quick to jump from Good Friday to Easter Sunday that I rarely contemplate what life must have been like for those earliest followers on that Holy Saturday. Yet in the quiet darkness of that day, a miracle was occurring, as all the power of evil and death was being undone. Teach me that you continue to work in hidden and unseen ways which you will reveal to me in your timing. Thank you for dying, for giving yourself up on my behalf. Show me the wisdom of waiting patiently for your return. In your saving name I pray. Amen.

day40

LUKE 24:1–8

On the first day of the week, very early in the morning, the women took the spices they had prepared and went to the tomb. They found the stone rolled away from the tomb, but when they entered, they did not find the body of the Lord Jesus. While they were wondering about this, suddenly two men in clothes that gleamed like lightning stood beside them. In their fright the women bowed down with their faces to the ground, but the men said to them, "Why do you look for the living among the dead? He is not here; he has risen! Remember how he told you, while he was still with you in Galilee: 'The Son of Man must be delivered over to the hands of sinners, be crucified and on the third day be raised again.'" Then they remembered his words.

READ ALSO 1 CORINTHIANS 15:1–6,17–22.

MEDITATION

All of Christianity is summed up in one verifiable historical event. And this changes everything. Jesus of Nazareth, a maverick Jewish rabbi and prophet, who claimed to be the Messiah about whom Scripture foretold, was arrested, condemned in an illegal trial and crucified. A soldier's spear to his side and the blood and water that flowed from the wound confirmed that his lungs had collapsed. He was dead. Days after his body had been prepared and placed in a sealed tomb, some women went back to the tomb and found the Roman seal broken, the stone rolled away from the entrance and his body (along with the guards whose lives depended on their keeping watch over it) gone. Soon after that day, more than 500 people claimed to have seen him alive. Others claimed to have seen him ascend into heaven. Most of these witnesses were still alive at the time of the writing of the four Gospels. If the words of this "Good News" were not true, one of those witnesses would have surely refuted them.

Those who committed to follow Jesus early on gained no visible benefit from following him, no wealth or power or possession. Rather, many were themselves beaten, stoned, tortured and crucified. Yet Christianity has persisted on through history to today. And because we know that this account of Jesus' death and resurrection is factual, we can also know that his promises are sure. The One who died as a criminal to take our sin away from us is alive now, preparing a place for us. And one day, we will be made alive again with him.   ✤

PRAYER

Loving Lord, you have called us to be born again to a living hope that comes through the resurrection of Jesus Christ. You are preparing an inheritance for me that will never be corrupted and never fade away. And yet I confess that I often put my hope in other things. Deliver me from the futility of misplaced hopes. Teach me the wisdom of seeking you and finding security in your unchanging character. Only your promises will stand forever. It is folly to trust in people, possessions or position because all of these ultimately disappoint. Instead, I place my hope in you. I pray that I will grow in knowing, loving and trusting you. In Jesus' name I pray. Amen.